I0820087

First published in the US in 2026 by
Welbeck Children's Books
An imprint of Hachette Children's Group

Author: Emily Stead
Designer: Jonathan Finch

ISBN 978 1 80453 925 5

Printed in China
10 9 8 7 6 5 4 3 2 1

Welbeck Children's Books
An imprint of Hachette Children's Group
Part of Hodder & Stoughton Limited
Carmelite House, 50 Victoria Embankment
London EC4Y 0DZ

An Hachette UK Company
www.hachette.co.uk
www.hachettechildrens.co.uk

The publishers would like to thank the following sources for their kind permission to reproduce the pictures in this book.

Getty Images: Aitor Alcalde/FIFA 74BR; Gabriel Aponte 51TR; Raul Arboleda/AFP 51BL; Ayman Aref/NurPhoto 33BL; Chris Arjoon/AFP 68BL; Gonzalo Arroyo/FIFA 75BR; Naomi Baker 34TR; Naomi Baker/The FA 26L; Robbie Jay Barratt/AMA 59BR; Al Bello 43TL; Daniel Beloumou Olomo/AFP 54TR; Shaun Botterill 27TR; Karl Bridgeman/The FA 6-7; Chris Brunskill/Fantasista 30TR; Simon Bruty/Anychance 36R; Alex Burstow/Arsenal FC 10T[illegible]; Giuseppe Cacace/AFP 55TR; Rodrigo Caillaud/Eurasia Sport Images 50B; Lynne Cameron/The FA 49TL; Alex Caparros/FIFA 74L; Ramsey Cardy/Sportsfile/UEFA 71BL; Jean Catuffe 28TR, 66B; Chung Sung-Jun 55BL; Piero Cruciatti/AFP 64TR; Carl de Souza/AFP 44R; Oscar Del Pozo/AFP 60L; Daniel Derajinski/Icon Sport 67TR; Tony Duffy/Allsport 35TR; Elsa 26R; Elsa/NWSL 69TR; Franck Fife/AFP 41, 42TR, 44BL, 46BR, 47TL, 66L, 77; Julian Finney/UEFA 4, 70BL; Toni Galan 73TR; Ewen Gavet/Icon Sport 67BL; James Gill/Danehouse 19BL; Alex Gottschalk/DeFodi Images 39T; Rich Graessle/Icon Sportswire 29TR; Pascal Guyot/AFP 21TR; Matthias Hangst 62L; Morgan Harlow/The FA 59BL; Image Photo Agency 64C, 65BR; Catherine Ivill/AMA 29BL; Catherine Ivill/UEFA 71TR; Daniel Jayo 42BR; Kirill Kudryavtsev/AFP 43[illegible]L, 76; Harriet Lander/Chelsea FC 28L; Harriet Lander/FIFA 46L; Philippe Le Tellier/Paris Match 35L; Andy Lyons 27BL; Stuart MacFarlane/Arsenal FC 57; Marcio Machado/Eurasia Sport Images 10BR; David Madison 53BR; Jure Makovec/AFP 32TR; Matt McNulty/UEFA 38R; Melinda Meijer/ISI Photos 68TR; Indranil Mukherjee/AFP 55L; Guang Niu 34BR; Christina Pahnke/sampics 62BR; Alex Pantling/UEFA 48; John Peters/Manchester United 58BL; Matthew Peters/Manchester United 35BR; Popperfoto 9TL, 9TR, 9C; Daniela Porcelli 45T, 63B; Daniela Porcelli/ISI Photos 47B; Stefan Postles 65T[illegible]; David Price/Arsenal FC 13BR, 58TR, 72; Manuel Queimadelos/Quality Sport Images 61L, 70TR; Ben Radford /Allsport 54BC; David Ramos 19TR, 34BL, 61R; David Ramos/FIFA 73BL; Ben Roberts Photo 39L; Sandra Ruhaut/Icon Sport 75T; Fadel Senna/AFP 60BR; Justin Setterfield 23B; Ezra Shaw 20, 80; Brad Smith/ISI Photos 53TR; Andreas Solaro/AFP 6[illegible]R; Andrea Staccioli/Insidefoto/LightRocket 15TR; Catherine Steenkeste 16-17; Rich Storry/NWSL 69BR; Selim Sudheimer 63TR; Bob Thomas Sports Photography 9BR, 22TR; Mark Thompson 31BR; John Todd/ISI Photos 38B; Pius Utomi Ekpei/AFP 54BR; Joan Valls/Urbanandsport/NurPhoto 31L; Omar Vega 52; Claudio Villa 24-25, 27L; Visionhaus 58B[illegible]; Darren Walsh/Chelsea FC 22BL, 36L; William West/AFP 33TR; Sebastian Widmann/UEFA 21BR; James Worsfold 18L; Mustafa Yalcin/Anadolu Agency 33BR

Shutterstock: BRG.photography 23L; Dedraw Studio 1, 3, 26B, 28B, 30B, 32B; Eugene B[illegible]sov 50TR; Golden Sikorka 11BL; grey_and 27TL; Jackreznor 11TR; Nattawit Khomsanit 15TL; Kotoimages 14; Igor K[illegible]ytsya 31TR; Alberto Martin/EPA 21BL; Master1305 13T; Member 11L; MockupMonster 15BL; moondes 10TL; [illegible]atrot 37L, 37R, 37BL, 37BR; A.Paes 13BL; Refox Photos 15BR, 18R; SL-Photography 8; vectorlight 45B; Yuri A/PeopleImages 23TR

Every effort has been made to acknowledge correctly and contact the source and/or copyright holder of each picture and Welbeck Publishing Group apologises for any unintentional errors or omissions, which will be corrected in future editions of this book.

The Junior SOCCER Encyclopedia

WELBECK
CHILDREN'S BOOKS

Contents

MANCHESTER CITY
Emirates FA CUP
ORTEGA
WALKER
DIAS
STONES
GUNDOGAN
HAALAND
GREALISH
RODRIGO
SILVA
AKANJI
FODEN
2-1
83:47

The beautiful game

Soccer, which is called football outside of the US, is the world's most popular sport! Huge crowds travel to see soccer games played in stadiums, with many more fans watching on TV. Two teams, each with 11 players, must kick a ball into a goal to score. The team that scores the most goals wins the game.

How soccer began

People have played ball games for thousands of years, all over the world. Many of these games helped to shape how soccer is played today. Here's how...

3,000 years ago

The ancient Maya people played a game called "pitz." Players scored by passing a rubber ball through a carved stone hoop using their arms or hips.

2,000 years ago

"Cuju" was a game played long ago in China. The name means "kick-ball." Players had to kick a leather ball stuffed with feathers.

2,800 years ago

"Episkyros" was played by the Ancient Greeks. It is an early form of soccer, but players could use their arms to move the ball.

900 years ago

In medieval England, whole villages of peasants joined in to kick an inflated pig's bladder. Matches were so noisy that King Edward II banned London games in 1314!

200 years ago

Pupils in some English schools in the 19th century played a game that was a cross between modern soccer and rugby. Every school had its own set of rules.

over 150 years ago

In October 1863, the rules of modern soccer were written down for the first time by the English Football Association. One important rule was that players could not carry the ball with their hands!

Soccer first

The first international game was played between Scotland and England in Glasgow, Scotland, in 1872. Up to four thousand fans came to watch at Hamilton Crescent cricket ground. The score was 0–0.

In the early days of soccer, players wore woollen stockings, long pants and thick cotton jerseys.

INTERNATIONAL
FOOT-BALL MATCH,
(ASSOCIATION RULES,)
ENGLAND v. SCOTLAND,
WEST OF SCOTLAND CRICKET GROUND,
HAMILTON CRESCENT, PARTICK,
SATURDAY, 30th November, 1872, at 2 p.m.
ADMISSION—ONE SHILLING.

A growing game

Toward the end of the 19th century, workers who traveled around the British Empire introduced soccer to countries in Africa, South America, Asia, and beyond. More countries began to organize their own competitions.

Did you know?

Asian nations Japan and Siam (now Thailand) entered the first World Cup in 1930, held in Uruguay, but decided not to play. Egypt missed the tournament as their ship was late because of a storm!

Women's soccer

Can you believe it? In the 20th century, women were banned from playing professional soccer in many countries for around 50 years! Now women's soccer is growing again, with more professional leagues and competitions than ever before. More than 30 million women and girls now play soccer around the world.

The United States won the first Women's World Cup in 1991, more than 60 years after the men's tournament was first held.

Soccer rules

Many of the rules of soccer were first written down in 1863, by the English FA. More rules have been added over the years.

Substitutes

Up to five more players can join the game as substitutes. They replace teammates who are injured or tired, or are brought on to help the team's tactics. Substitutes sit in seats known as the bench.

Teams

Each team is made up of 11 players. One is a goalkeeper and the other ten are called **outfield** players. Matches cannot be played with fewer than seven players a side.

Coaching staff

The coach or manager is in charge of the team. They pick which players to play and decide the game tactics. Assistant coaches and a medical team are part of the coaching staff too.

Did you know?

Carlo Ancelotti is the only manager to win all five of Europe's top leagues, in Italy, England, France, Spain, and Germany.

The field of play

A soccer field is rectangular and marked with white lines. Soccer fields can be different sizes, but they need to be a certain size for professional games. The playing surface is most often grass, but artificial turf is popular too.

The length of the field must measure between 90 and 120 meters (100–130 yards), and its width between 45 and 90 meters (50–100 yards).

Tall floodlights in stadiums mean that games can be played safely at night.

Under-soil heating

Many fields around the world have under-soil heating below the playing surface. Hot water travels through pipes, which stops the field from freezing during cold weather.

Soccer rules

The referee

The referee makes sure that the game is played according to the rules. They have a whistle to attract the players' attention, and a stopwatch to time the game correctly. They write important facts about the game in a notebook.

Cards

The referee can show a yellow or red card to any player who commits a serious foul.

The yellow card is a warning. The player can play on, but two yellow cards means an automatic red card.

The player must leave the field immediately, and cannot return.

A straight red card can be shown without a yellow card first.

Assistant referees

Two assistant referees run up and down the **touchlines** and carry a flag. They help the main referee and can talk to them through a headset. They help decide throw-ins and when players are offside. A fourth official is in charge of substitutions.

VAR

Some competitions have an extra Video Assistant Referee (VAR). This referee watches video clips of the game to check that the referee on the field has made the right decision.

Goal or no goal?

Cameras in the goal record when the ball has crossed the goal line. A signal is sent to the referee's watch to tell them whether or not a goal should be awarded. This is called goal line technology (GLT).

Soccer gear

Soccer players don't need a lot of expensive equipment to play the sport they love. Here is some of the basic gear.

shirt and shorts

Soccer uniforms are made from lightweight fabrics that are comfortable to move around in and that keep players cool and dry.

socks

Long socks that can hold shin pads in place.

ball

In professional soccer, balls must be a certain size and weight. Younger players play with smaller-sized balls, depending on how old they are.

cleats

Soccer Players wear special cleats with studs on the sole to help grip the field. Studs are usually made from plastic or metal. Players choose which type of cleats to wear according to the surface of the field.

base layers

In cold weather, tops and leggings called base layers or skins can be worn underneath the soccer uniform. They help keep to muscles warm and avoid injuries, and move sweat away from the body.

Did you know?

Some uniforms are made from recycled polyester, using recycled plastic bottles.

water bottle

Water is the best drink to replace the fluids lost while playing soccer. Not drinking enough water can make players **dehydrated**. Fizzy or sugary drinks are not good choices when playing sports.

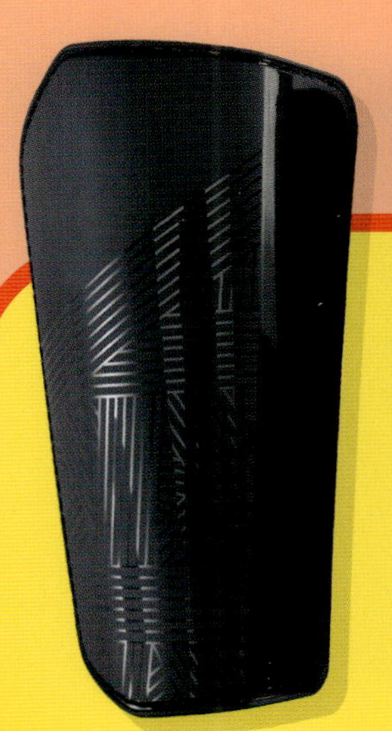

shin pads

These are designed to protect the shin bone from contact with the ball and from other players. All players must wear shin pads to prevent injuries.

1 Soccer skills

Soccer players need to learn a range of skills if they want to become professional players. It takes years of working on skills like passing, shooting, tackling, dribbling, and heading in training to reach the very top. The best soccer players are superb at controlling the ball.

10

Ball control, passing, and shooting are three key skills that players must learn from a young age. Working hard on these skills in training helps players to be at their best when playing games.

Ball control

Being able to control the ball well is important whatever your position on the field. The best players are comfortable controlling the ball with both feet and can use different parts of the foot.

The chest, thighs, and head are also used to control the ball, bringing it close to the feet before making a pass or taking a shot.

Passing

Passing the ball between teammates is the best way to keep possession. Players move the ball up the field until they create a chance to score. Passes can be made on the ground or in the air.

Did you know?

Some teams make more than 1,000 passes during a match!

Accuracy

Striking through the center of the ball with the inside of the shooting foot makes shots more accurate.

Shooting

Shooting is when a player strikes the ball at goal. Players can take shots from anywhere on the field, but shots inside the penalty area are more likely to be on target. Shots also include headers on goal.

Power

To create power in their shots, players often hit the ball with the top of the foot (where the laces are). After kicking the ball, their shooting leg follows through in the direction of the goal.

Did you know?

The fastest shots in soccer can reach speeds of up to 131 miles per hour (210 km per hour).

Dribbling, tackling, and heading the ball are three more important skills that players use in training and in games.

Dribbling

Dribbling is the skill of moving the ball while running, taking small touches to move it forwards up the field. Players need to have good ball control and be skilled at using both feet.

Head up

Players should keep their head up while dribbling, so they don't run into danger.

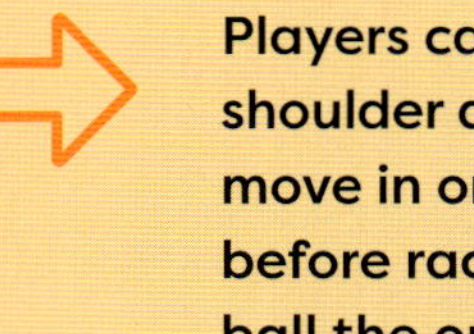

Shoulder switch

Players can drop a shoulder and pretend to move in one direction, before racing off with the ball the opposite way.

Fast feet

Strong dribblers take lots of touches using the inside and outside of their feet to control the ball.

Tackling

Tackling is when a player wins the ball from an opponent. Even defenders don't make many tackles in a match, but when they do, they must take the ball without giving away a foul or causing an injury.

Being aware

Players need to watch their opponent, the space around them, and where the ball is before, during, and after making the tackle.

Timing the tackle

The player needs to be close enough to make contact with enough of the ball to win it cleanly and safely.

Heading

Heading the ball in the air is an important skill for players in any position. Defensive headers can stop goals while attackers use their heads to score goals. Headers are not practiced in youth soccer to keep players safe.

Making contact

Players connect with the ball using their forehead for power and accuracy, at the highest point of their jump.

Did you know?

Cristiano Ronaldo holds the record for the highest headed goal in soccer history. He leaped 9 ft 7 in (2.93 m) to score in the UEFA Champions League in 2012-2013.

Set pieces

Set pieces are used to restart the game following a foul, or after the ball goes out of play. Attacking set pieces give teams a good chance to score a goal, especially through free kicks and penalty kicks.

Free kicks

A free kick can be awarded anywhere on the field following a foul. If the ball is close enough to the goal, a player on the attacking side may try to shoot. The free-kick taker may also pass the ball to a teammate. The defending team often makes a wall of players to try to block the ball.

Did you know?

A goal scored directly from a corner kick without touching any other players is called an "Olimpico".

Corner kicks

A corner kick is awarded to the attacking team if the ball last touches a player of the defending team before going out of play behind the goal line. The whole of the ball must pass over the goal line.

Corner kicks are taken within the white arc in the corner of the field. Any player can score from a corner, even the goalkeeper of the attacking team!

Cole Palmer takes a corner kick for Chelsea in the Premier League.

Throw-ins

When the ball goes out of play over either touchline, a throw-in is taken to restart play. Keeping both feet on the ground, players must throw the ball from behind their head using both hands.

Penalty kicks

A penalty kick is awarded when a foul by the defending team takes place within the penalty area. These are one-on-one shots against the goalkeeper.

Penalty shootout

A penalty shootout is often used when the score is a draw in a tournament, to decide who wins. A shootout often takes place after a period of extra time.

Each team takes five penalty kicks. If the scores are still even after this, teams take more penalty kicks in turn until one team wins.

2 Field positions

Soccer teams are made up of 11 players, who take their places in different positions on the field. Each player has their own job to do to help the team. Teams have one goalkeeper, while the other ten players are a mix of defenders, midfielders, and forwards.

9

FIELD POSITIONS

Goalkeepers

A goalkeeper is only the only player on the team who is allowed to use their hands to touch the ball, but only in their own penalty area. They need to be good with their hands as well as their feet to stop the ball from hitting the back of their net. They are sometimes called the "last line of defense."

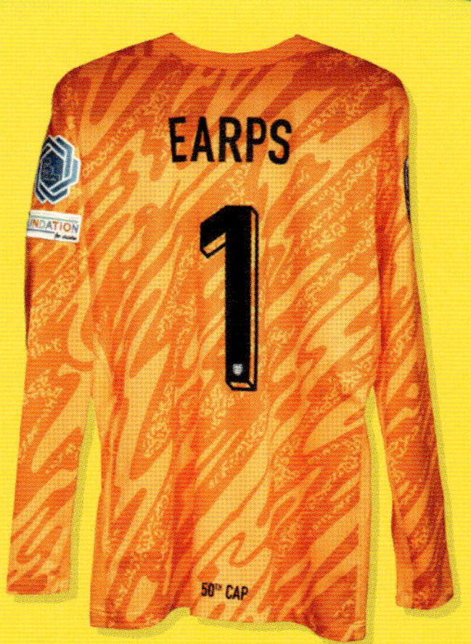

Keeper's uniform

Goalkeepers wear a different colored jersey from their teammates so the referee can see who has handled the ball in a crowd of players. The number on the back is often 1 or 13.

Emi Martínez was voted the best goalkeeper in the world 2024 and the second best in 2023.

Top skills

- Shot-stopping
- Catching crosses
- Diving
- Kicking out
- Throwing
- Quick reflexes

Special gloves help goalkeepers grip the ball and protect their hands and wrists from injuries.

Alisson Becker's quick thinking and perfect passes create chances for his teammates to score.

Staying alert

Goalkeepers sometimes don't touch the ball for long periods of time during a match. They must stay focused and be ready to make a save. Keepers can start a quick attack for their own side too, by launching a long throw or kick to catch opponents off guard.

Cleaning up

USA goalkeeper Alyssa Naeher kept **clean sheets** in the finals of both the 2019 World Cup and the Paris 2024 Olympics to help her country become champions.

Did you know?

Goalkeepers don't need to run around as much as other players during a match. The energy they save over the years means they often have a longer soccer career than their teammates.

Defenders

Defenders have the job of stopping their opponents from scoring a goal. Teams can play with three, four, or five defenders depending on their **tactics**. There are different types of defenders: central defenders, full-backs, sweepers, and wing-backs who line up together in front of the goalkeeper.

Netherlands captain Virgil van Dijk is one of the world's most skillful defenders. He plays in central defense.

Worth a million

In January 2025, USA central defender Naomi Girma made history by becoming the first female soccer player to cost over $1 million. Her move from San Diego Wave to Chelsea set a new world record in the women's game.

Top skills

- Tackling
- Passing
- Heading
- Clearing the ball
- Positioning
- Strength

Quick as a flash

Sometimes a team's quickest players play in defense. Left-back Alphonso Davies is known for his incredible speed when defending and attacking down the **wing.**

Lionesses legend

Lucy Bronze is a right wing-back who loves to help the attack. She has played more than 130 matches for England's Lionesses and scored more than 15 goals, too.

Did you know?

Defenders, and center-backs in particular, make excellent team captains. They have a good view of the whole field and can shout instructions to their teammates.

Midfielders

Midfielders play between their team's defenders and forwards, in the middle of the field. There are different types of midfielder, but all must have strong passing skills and plenty of energy. The number of midfielders in a team depends on its formation.

Spain and Manchester City midfielder Rodri is a master at winning the ball in midfield for club and country.

Defensive duties

The job of a defensive midfielder is to break up the opposition's attack. They must read the game well to predict how teams will try to move forwards with the ball. They try to stop passes and make important tackles. They play just in front of their team's defense.

Wide midfielder

Wide midfielders play close to the touchline on either the left or the right of the field. They make chances for other players to score by putting crosses into the box, or they take shots themselves.

Top skills

- Passing
- Tackling
- Ball control
- Dribbling
- Creativity
- Positioning

Midfield engine

A central midfielder operates in the middle of the field. They are sometimes called the "engine" of the team as they work hard to link the defense and the attack. They make lots of passes during a match and often do the most running over a game.

This heatmap shows where this midfielder spent their time during a game. The red areas are where they spent the most time.

On the attack

Attacking midfielders are often the team's most creative players. They need to be good at all different types of passes to create chances for their teammates to score. Central attacking midfielders are sometimes called "playmakers."

Playmaker Aitana Bonmatí has won the Ballon d'Or trophy twice.

Did you know?

Midfielder David Beckham's crossing skills were so good, they inspired the name of a film: *Bend It Like Beckham*!

Forwards

The forwards on a team have the task of creating and scoring goals. There are different types of forwards. The center forward or striker plays farthest forward, wingers attack down the left and right and sides of the field, and the second striker (No.10) plays in the space behind the main striker.

Super striker

Striker Erling Haaland may not make many touches during a match, but his goal-scoring record is among the best players in history.

Did you know?

In modern soccer, forwards must also help defend. They try to stop the opposition's goalkeeper and defenders from moving the ball up the field.

Top skills

Shooting	Dribbling
Heading	Speed
Crossing	Agility

Goal queen

Khadija "Bunny" Shaw is Jamaica's all-time top goalscorer for both the women's and men's teams. She holds the ball up well and has a deadly strike.

Kylian Mbappé won the Golden Boot at the 2022 World Cup in Qatar. His eight goals helped France reach the final.

Wing wonder

Egypt's Mohamed Salah scores a fantastic amount of goals playing on the right wing. Not only is his shooting deadly, but he is responsible for many **assists** for his teammates.

Golden boot

Many tournaments and leagues award a special trophy called the Golden Boot (or Shoe) to the player that has scored the most goals during the competition.

Record breakers

Since the modern game began, fans around the world have watched their heroes achieve some incredible feats in soccer. Many records have stood for decades and may never be beaten.

Most international goals
(men or women)

190

Christine Sinclair
(Canada)

Most goals in a calendar year

91

Lionel Messi
(Barcelona), in 2012

Most international appearances
(men or women)

354

Kristine Lilly
(United States)

Youngest World Cup winner

17 years and **249** days old

Pelé (Brazil),
1958 tournament

Most clean sheets
(all seasons)

537

Ray Clemence
(Scunthorpe Utd, Liverpool, and Tottenham Hotspur), from 1965–88

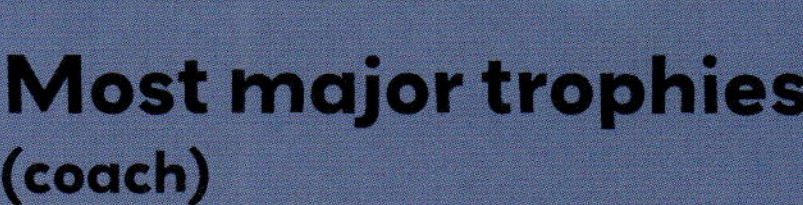

Most major trophies
(coach)

49

Alex Ferguson

Most international trophies

22

Argentina

3 World Cup wins
16 Copa América wins
1 Confederations Cup champions win
2 CONMEBOL–UEFA Cup wins

Tactics and formations

Soccer coaches choose different tactics and formations to try to get the best result in a match.

Team tactics

Teams that have good technical players often focus on keeping hold of the ball and passing it around. This is called keeping **possession**.

Some teams play **counter-attacking** soccer. Instead of trying to keep possession, they use their speedy players to quickly launch an attack when their opponents lose the ball.

Other teams play a more **direct** style of soccer. Instead of making lots of passes from the defense to midfield to the forwards, long balls are launched from the goalkeeper or defense towards the forwards. The forwards use their strength and height to try to win the ball.

Coaches can change their tactics during a game if they need to.

Four formations

A formation is how a team is set up on the field, broken down into rows of defenders, midfielders, and forwards. For 11-a-side soccer, the numbers add up to 10. The goalkeeper is not included.

What do the numbers mean?

4 - 3 - 3

The number of defenders.

The number of midfielders.

The number of forwards.

4–3–3

This formation is often used by many of the world's top teams. It is a more attacking formation with three forwards who can create more chances to score.

4–4–2

A classic formation that gives teams a good balance in defense and attack. It is not as popular as it once was, but many teams still line up this way.

4–2–3–1

This set-up is more defensive, with four defenders and two defensive midfielders. Three attacking midfielders and a striker complete the line-up.

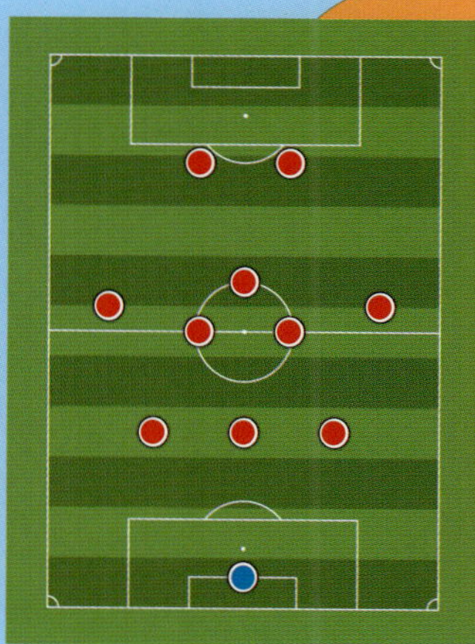

3–5–2

Three central defenders form a strong defense. Two wing-backs are part of a midfield five, while two strikers try to score.

Super stadiums

Fans have gathered in stadiums to watch sports for thousands of years. Today, clubs and national teams have their own modern stadiums so that thousands of fans can come and watch games. Some stadiums can seat more than 100,000 fans!

Did you know?

The modern Wembley Stadium was built on the same site as the original stadium that had stood from 1923 until 2003. It reopened in 2007 with 90,000 seats. It is home to England's men's and women's national teams.

USA's largest soccer stadium

The Rose Bowl in California is a huge stadium that can hold up to 92,000 spectators. It hosts all kinds of sports including baseball and football, but it's most famous in the soccer world for hosting the 1994 World Cup final.

Shared stadium

The most famous stadium shared by two teams can be found in Milan, Italy. The San Siro stadium (also called the Stadio Giuseppe Meazza) has been the home ground of both AC Milan and Internazionale since 1947.

Oldest stadium

The world's oldest soccer stadium that is still used today is Sandygate in Sheffield, England. The first competitive game played at the ground took place on December 26, 1860. The two teams were Hallam and Sheffield FC.

Sky-high stadium

The Estadio Daniel Alcides Carrión in Cerro de Pasco, Peru, is the highest altitude stadium in the world. It was built 14,370 ft (4,380 m) above sea level. Playing soccer is difficult there, as there is less oxygen to breathe.

3 Top tournaments

Some of the biggest tournaments and prizes in sport belong to soccer. The ultimate tournament in both the men's and women's games is the World Cup, while each continent has its own competition to decide a champion. Soccer is an Olympic sport too, with the chance for players to win more medals for their country.

ENGLAND
20 AUGUST 2023
SYDNEY
FIFA WOMEN'S WORLD CUP AU·NZ·2023
ENGLAND
20 AUGUST 2023
SYDNEY

The World Cup

The biggest competition in soccer is the World Cup. It's a celebration of the beautiful game, with international teams from across the globe battling to win the famous trophy. Up to 48 teams will be competing in the 2026 World Cup. Every player dreams of winning the World Cup!

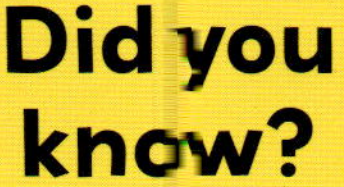

Did you know?

Winners of the trophy get a star sewn above the crest on their shirt for each World Cup victory. This is Brazil's famous canary yellow shirt.

Amazing Brazil

Brazil has won the World Cup a record five times. Italy and Germany each have four trophies.

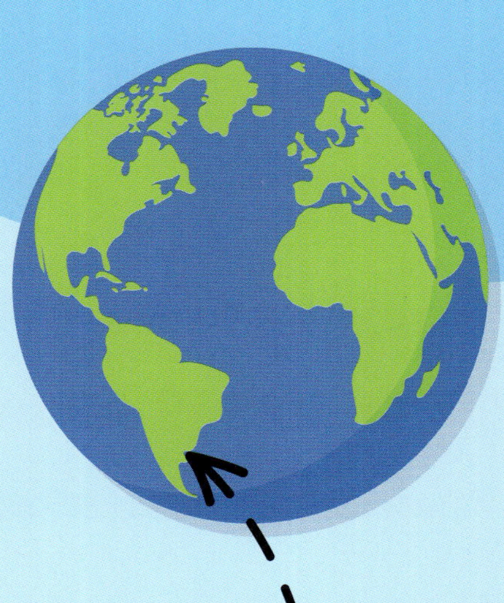

Kicking off

The first men's World Cup was held in Uruguay, South America, in 1930. The home team was the very first winners.

Argentina became the men's champion for the third time when it won the 2022 World Cup. Argentina's superstar captain was Lionel Messi.

Triple header

Three nations were chosen to host the World Cup in 2026 together: the United States, Canada, and Mexico. The MetLife Stadium in New Jersey was selected to stage the final.

Billions of fans

More than 5 billion people watched the 2022 World Cup on TV or online. That's more than half the world's population! Close to 1.5 billion fans watched the final between Argentina and France.

Portugal's Cristiano Ronaldo became the first man to score at five different World Cups at the 2022 tournament.

World Cup records

Most wins

5 - Brazil

Winning nations

Uruguay, Italy, Germany, Brazil, England, Argentina, France, Spain

Most appearances
(tournaments)

5 - Lionel Messi (Argentina)
5 - Lothar Matthäus (Germany)
5 - Cristiano Ronaldo (Portugal)
5 - Rafael Marquez (Mexico)
5 - Andres Guardado (Mexico)

Most appearances
(games)

26 - Lionel Messi (Argentina)

Top scorer (all)

16 goals - Miroslav Klose (Germany)

Top scorer (single tournament)

13 goals - Just Fontaine (France)

The Women's World Cup

Just like the men's competition, the Women's World Cup is the biggest tournament in women's soccer. It was first held in 1991 and was won by the United States. Nine tournaments have been played so far, with 32 nations now competing for World Cup glory.

Winning nations

The USA has a fantastic record at the Women's World Cup and has been crowned champion a record four times. Germany has two titles, and Japan and Norway have one each. Spain's women won their first trophy in 2023.

Spain beat England 1–0 in the final of the World Cup 2023 in Sydney, Australia.

Did you know?

The trophy awarded to the winners is not the original cup. The first trophy was stolen after Norway won it in 1995. The current cup, made from gold-plated brass, has been used since the 1999 tournament.

World Cup records

Most wins

4 - United States

Winning nations

United States, Germany, Japan, Norway, Spain

Most appearances (tournaments)

7 - Formiga (Brazil)

Most appearances (games)

30 - Kristine Lilly (United States)

Top scorer (all)

17 goals - Marta (Brazil)

Top scorer (single tournament)

10 goals - Michelle Akers (United States)

Brazil teammates Marta and Formiga are both former World Cup record-breakers.

Global game

Australia and New Zealand hosted the 2023 Women's World Cup together. This was the first time the tournament was held in the Southern Hemisphere and by two countries. Brazil will host the 2027 competition, making it the first tournament to be played in South America.

The Olympic Games

Soccer became an Olympic sport at the Paris 1900 Games, decades before the first World Cup. A men's tournament has been played at every Games since, except one. The first time women were able to compete for an Olympic medal came much later, at the Atlanta 1996 games.

Tournament rules

Many famous male soccer players don't play in the Olympic tournament. Instead, nations must choose young players under the age of 23 for their squads, with three over-23s allowed.

Going for gold

Shiny gold medals are awarded to the winners, the runners-up earn silver, and the nation to finish in third place wins bronze medals

Spain's young stars won the country's first gold medal since 1992 at the Paris 2024 Games.

Gold rush

In the women's tournament, players of any age may play. Expect to see some of the world's best female soccer players. In the eight tournaments played so far, the United States has won gold five times, including at the first ever competition in Atlanta 1996. They have won a silver and a bronze medal too.

Mallory Swanson struck the winning goal as USA beat Brazil in the final at Paris 2024 to win gold.

Olympic soccer records

Most gold medals

Men: Hungary, Great Britain – **both 3**

Women: United States – **5**

Most medals

Men: Brazil – **7**

Women: United States – **7**

Most games played

Men: Brazil – **66**

Women: United States – **44**

Top scorer (all tournaments)

Men: Sophus Nielsen (Denmark) and Antal Dunai (Hungary) – **both 13 goals**

Women: Cristiane (Brazil) – **14 goals**

Top scorer (single tournaments)

Men: Ferenc Bene (Hungary) – **12 goals**

Women: Vivianne Miedema (Netherlands) – **10 goals**

Did you know?

Brazil's women's team has lost three Olympic finals, defeated each time by the United States.

Brazil defender Tamires shows off her silver medal from the Paris 2024 Games.

Europe

Both the European Championship and the Women's European Championship (called the Euros and Women's Euros for short) take place every four years. Nations compete to become champions of Europe, with 24 (men's) or 16 (women's)best international teams taking part in each tournament.

Top ten

Ten different teams have won the men's trophy since the competition began in 1960. Spain, Germany, Italy, and France have all won multiple titles, while the Soviet Union, Czechoslovakia, Netherlands, Denmark, Greece, and Portugal have each won once.

Spain is the current men's champion. They beat England 2–1 in the final of Euro 2024 in Germany.

Did you know?

England, the Republic of Ireland, Scotland, and Wales will jointly host the next tournament, which will kick off in 2028.

Women's winners

Only five countries have ever won the Women's Euros. They are Germany, Norway, Sweden, Netherlands, and England. Germany leads the way with eight trophies, winning the tournament six times in a row between 1995 and 2013. Norway is the next best nation with two trophies.

Lionesses roar to victory

When England hosted the Women's Euro 2022, their team nicknamed the Lionesses won every match they played. It was a dream come true to win their very first trophy at the famous Wembley Stadium in London.

Euros records

Most wins (tournaments)

Men: Spain – **4**

Women: Germany – **8**

Most games played

Men: Germany – **58**

Women: Germany – **46**

Top scorer (all final tournaments)

Men: Cristiano Ronaldo (Portugal) – **14 goals**

Women: Inka Grings and Birgit Prinz (both Germany) – **10 goals**

Top scorer (single final tournaments)

Men: Michel Platini (France) – **9 goals**

Women: Inka Grings (Germany), Beth Mead (England), and Alexandra Popp (Germany) – **6 goals**

Did you know?

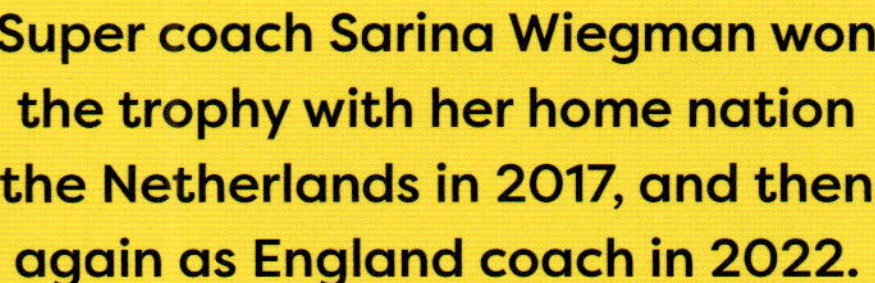

Super coach Sarina Wiegman won the trophy with her home nation the Netherlands in 2017, and then again as England coach in 2022.

South America

The men's Copa América is famous for being the oldest **continental** soccer competition that still runs today. The first tournament was held over a hundred years ago between four national teams from South America. Now 16 teams take part, with teams from other continents often invited to play.

Team triple

Only Argentina has won three Copa América tournaments in a row, between 1945 and 1947.

A plaque with the name of the winner is added to the base of the Copa América trophy after every final.

Copa América Femenina

The women's competition kicked off in 1991, with the host Brazil crowned the very first winner. Brazil has an almost perfect record in the competition, winning the trophy eight times altogether. In fact, Brazil has only ever lost the tournament once, when Argentina came out on top in the 2006 final.

Did you know?

In both men's and women's soccer, the Copa América champions play a one-off match against the European Champions for the chance to win the Finalissima trophy.

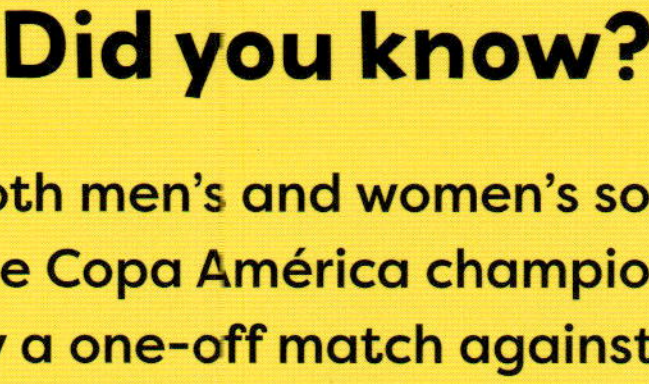

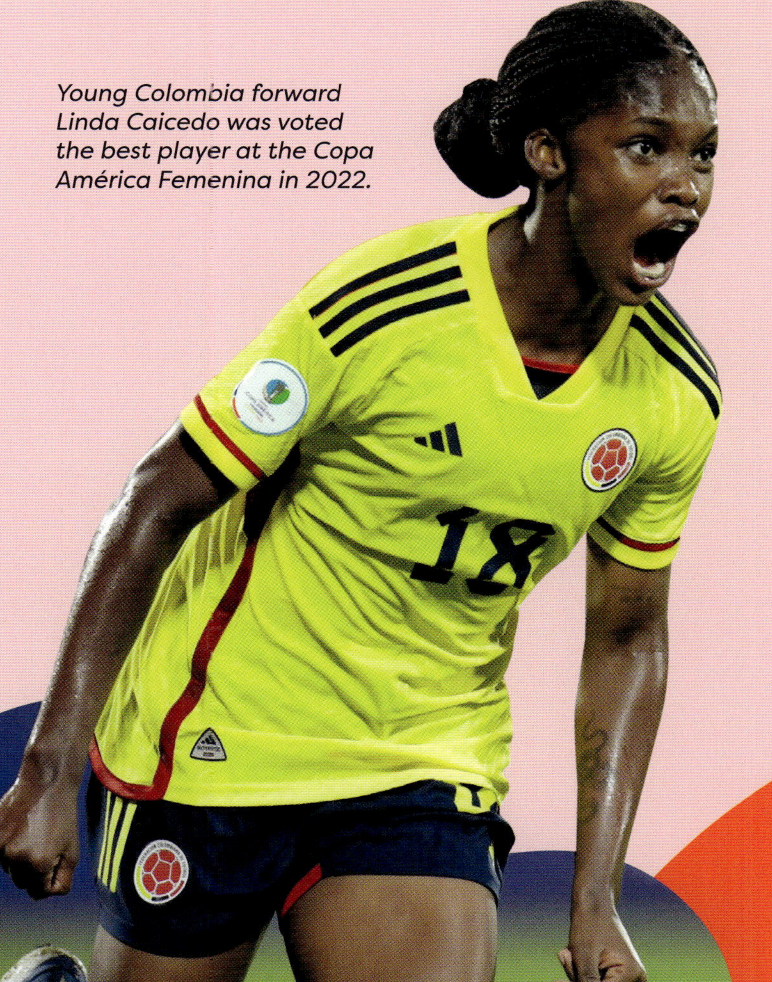

Young Colombia forward Linda Caicedo was voted the best player at the Copa América Femenina in 2022.

South America records

Most wins (tournaments)

Men: Argentina – 16

Women: Brazil – 8

Most games played (tournaments)

Men: Uruguay – 212

Women: Argentina and Brazil – 50

Most tournaments played (player)

Men: Lionel Messi (Argentina) – 39

Women: Formiga (Brazil) – 6

Top scorer (all tournaments)

Men: Norberto Méndez (Argentina) and Zizinho (Brazil) – **17 goals**

Women: Cristiane (Brazil) – **31 goals**

Top scorer (single tournaments)

Men: Jair (Brazil), Humberto Maschio (Argentina), and Javier Ambrois (Uruguay) – **9 goals**

Women: Roseli (Brazil) – **16 goals**

North and Central America

For countries in North America, Central America, and the Caribbean, the biggest tournament is called the Gold Cup. It is held every two years. Since the competition began in 1991, so far only three national teams have won it: the United States, Mexico, and Canada.

Magical Mexico

As of January 2025, Mexico held the record for the most tournament wins with nine titles. USA held seven titles and Canada had been champion once. All three nations are from North America.

Men's Gold Cup records

Most wins (tournaments)	Mexico – 9
Most games played (country)	Mexico – 125
Top scorer (all tournaments)	Landon Donovan (USA) – 18 goals
Top scorer (single tournament)	Luís Roberto Alves (Mexico) – 11 goals

Mexico beat Panama in the 2023 final to win the 2023 Gold Cup.

The United States beat rivals Canada to claim the 2022 cup.

CONCACAF W Championship records

Champions

United States – 9 times
Canada – 2 times

Runners-up

Canada – 6 times
Mexico – 2 times
Costa Rica, Brazil, and New Zealand – 1 each

Most games played (country)

United States – 44

Top scorer (single tournament)

Silvana Burtini (Canada) – 14 goals

CONCACAF W Championship

The biggest competition for women's national teams in North and Central America is the **CONCACAF** W Championship. The W stands for "Women's." It has been known by a few different names since the first edition in 1991. After a qualifying stage, eight nations compete in a knockout tournament to try to win the trophy. The winners also earn their place at the Women's World Cup.

Did you know?

Only the United States and Canada have ever won the Championship. The United States has a record nine triumphs, while Canada holds two titles.

Africa

The Africa Cup of Nations (AFCON) and women's cup (WAFCON) are the top trophies for national teams in Africa. The men's competition dates back to 1957, while the first women's edition was held in 1991. Teams compete from all across Africa.

Ivory Coast, nicknamed the Elephants, beat Nigeria in the 2023 final to win their third AFCON title.

African record-breakers

Most wins (tournaments)

Men: Egypt – 7

Women: Nigeria – 11

Winning nations
(more than one title)

Men: Egypt, Cameroon, Ghana, Nigeria, Ivory Coast, Algeria, DR Congo

Women: Nigeria, Equatorial Guinea

Top scorer
(single tournaments)

Men: Ndaye Mulamba (DR Congo) – **9 goals**

Women: Perpetua Nkwocha (Nigeria) – **11 goals**

Top scorer (all)

Men: Samuel Eto'o (Cameroon) – **18 goals**

Women: Perpetua Nkwocha (Nigeria) – **34 goals**

Most games

Rigobert Song holds the record for playing the most games at AFCON. The Cameroon defender played in the tournament 36 times and later became the team's coach.

Nigeria's Perpetua Nkwocha (right) is the all-time top scorer at WAFCON.

Asia

The first men's Asian Cup took place in Hong Kong in 1956 with only 4 Asian teams. A tournament for women's international teams followed in 1975. Today, up to 24 teams take part in the men's tournament, with 12 in the women's edition. Both competitions take place every four years.

Qatar won their second Asian Cup in 2023 as the competition's host nation.

Champions China

No team comes close to matching China's record in the Women's Asian Cup. Their record of nine titles is easily the best in the competition's history.

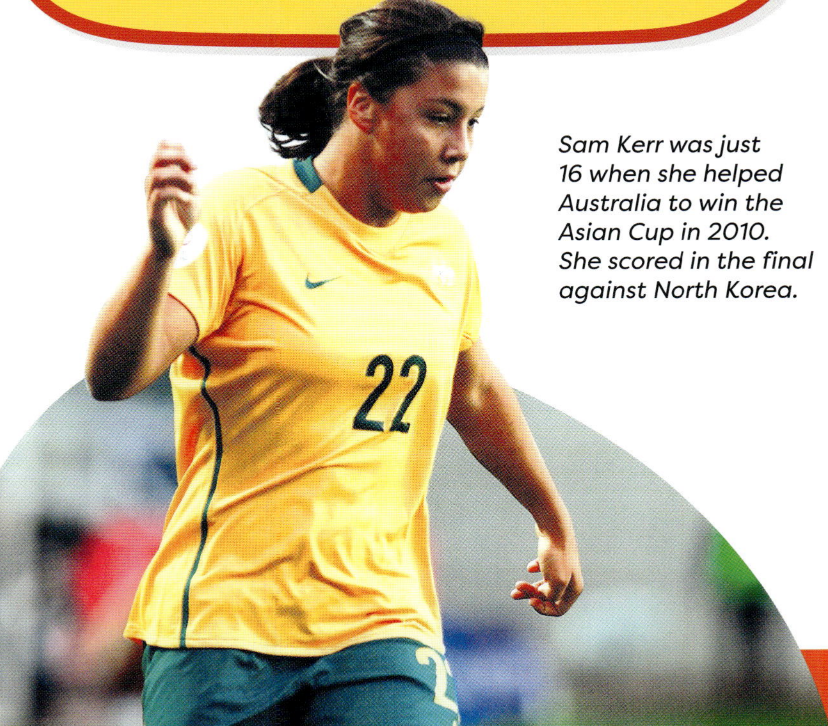

Sam Kerr was just 16 when she helped Australia to win the Asian Cup in 2010. She scored in the final against North Korea.

Asian Cup records

Most wins (tournaments)

Men: Japan – **4**

Women: China – **9**

Winning teams
(more than one title)

Men: Japan, Saudi Arabia, Iran, South Korea, Qatar

Women: China, North Korea, Chinese Taipei, Japan

Top scorer (single tournaments)

Men: Almoez Ali (Qatar) – **9 goals**

Women: Yūki Nagasato (Japan), Jung Jung-suk (Republic of Korea), Li Ying (China), Sam Kerr (Australia), Ri Kum-suk (DPRK) – **7 goals**

Top scorer (all)

Ali Daei (Iran) – **14 goals**

4

Soccer around the world

Soccer is the number one sport across the globe, with professional soccer played on every continent except Antarctica. The most famous men's and women's leagues are currently found in Europe. Some of the world's best players now star in the top leagues in United States and Saudi Arabia too.

Emirates
FLY BETTER

The Premier League

The top men's division in England is the Premier League. Its first season kicked off in 1992. Before that, the league was called the First Division. It's one of the fastest and most exciting leagues in the world. Many of the world's best players come to England to compete for the famous trophy.

Number of teams	20
Number of games each season	38
Clubs relegated each season	3

Premier League records

Most appearances
(all seasons)

Gareth Barry - 653 games

Top scorer
(all seasons)

Alan Shearer - 260

Most titles

Manchester United hold the record for the most Premier League titles won. They have been crowned champions 13 times. The last time they won the trophy was in the 2012–13 season.

Did you know?

Manchester City coach Pep Guardiola is the only coach to lead his side to win four Premier League titles in a row. He and City set the incredible record between 2021 and 2024.

The Women's Super League

The highest division in England for women is the Women's Super League (WSL). 14 professional teams play in the league. Each season, the top three teams qualify for the Women's Champions League.

Women's Super League records

Most appearances (all seasons)

Jordan Nobbs - **200+ games**

Top scorer (all seasons)

Vivianne Miedema - 80+

Number of teams	12
Number of games each season	22
Clubs relegated each season	1

Top for trophies

Since the league became the WSL in 2011, Chelsea have won the most titles. The London club won six straight titles between 2020 and 2025, a WSL record!

Did you know?

Midfielder Jordan Nobbs has played more WSL games than anyone else, playing for Arsenal and Aston Villa.

La Liga

The top men's league in Spain is called La Liga. It was first formed almost 100 years ago. Ten teams played in the first season in 1929. Today, double the number of teams compete, with the bottom three teams relegated to the second division at the end of each season.

La Liga records

Most appearances

(all seasons)

Andoni Zubizarreta and Joaquin both 622 games

Most points in a season

Real Madrid (2011–12) and Barcelona (2012–13) - 100

Top scorer

(all seasons)

Lionel Messi (Barcelona) - 474

Number of teams	20
Number of games each season	38
Clubs relegated each season	3

Kings of Spain

Real Madrid have won more La Liga titles than any other club. They have been champions more than 35 times. Barcelona are the next most successful club. Matches between these rival clubs are known as El Clásico (The Classic).

Real Madrid's riches allow them to buy the world's best players. Jude Bellingham's transfer fee was over one hundred million euros (about $114 million)!

Did you know?

Nine different teams have won La Liga's famous trophy.

Liga F

The Primera División de la Liga de Fútbol Femenino, known as Liga F for short, is the highest division for women's soccer in Spain. The league was founded in 1988 and it's now one of the most important women's leagues in Europe.

Number of teams	16
Number of games each season	30
Clubs relegated each season	2

Amazing Barça

Barcelona have won more titles than any other club. Their squad of superstars is made up of some of the best players in the women's game, from all over the world. The team is known for playing exciting, attacking soccer.

Did you know?

While twelve different clubs have been Liga F champions, Real Madrid has never won a title.

Midfielder Aitana Bonmatí has played for Barcelona since she joined their academy at the age of 13.

Liga F records

Most appearances

Barcelona – 32 seasons

Unbeaten in a season

Levante (2000–01) and Barcelona (2021–22)

Most Golden Boot trophies (all seasons)

Jenni Hermoso – 5

Bundesliga

Since Germany's top men's league began in 1963, 13 different clubs have been crowned champions. The soccer played is fast and physical, with the whole team working hard to win back the ball quickly if they lose it. Eighteen teams battle in the Bundesliga each season.

Bundesliga records

Most appearances (all seasons)

Karl-Heinz Körbel (Eintracht Frankfurt) - **602**

Most goals (all seasons)

Gerd Müller (Bayern Munich) - **365**

Most goals (in one seasons)

Robert Lewandowski - **41**

Number of teams	18
Number of games each season	34
Clubs relegated each season	2-3

German giants

Bayern Munich are easily the most successful Bundesliga team. They have won more than half the championships since the league began. Between 2013 and 2023, Bayern were champions a record 11 times in a row.

English striker Harry Kane joined Bayern Munich in 2023. He scored 36 goals in his first season at the club to earn the European Golden Shoe trophy.

Frauen-Bundesliga

In Germany, the top women's league is called the Frauen-Bundesliga. Fourteen teams compete from across the country, and the league boasts some of the strongest women's teams in Europe. Four different Frauen-Bundesliga clubs have won the Women's Champions League.

Number of teams	14
Number of games each season	22
Clubs relegated 2025 season	1

The Top Two

Over the last decade or so, two big clubs have ruled the competition—Bayern Munich and VfL Wolfsburg. They are always the favorites to win the league at the start of each season, as they almost always finish first and second.

Frauen-Bundesliga records

Most league titles
(all seasons)

FFC/Eintracht Frankfurt and VfL Wolfsburg – 7

Most goals (all seasons)

Kerstin Garefrekes - 211

Most goals (in one seasons)

Inka Grings (1999–2000) - 38

Many top players from other European countries star in the league, including English midfielder Georgia Stanway.

Serie A

The first season of Serie A began in Italy in 1929–30, almost one hundred years ago. The style of soccer played is more defensive than in other leagues and teams plan their tactics very carefully. It is considered to be one of the strongest leagues in the world. The Coppa Campioni d'Italia trophy is awarded to the winners.

Rivals AC Milan and Internazionale are two of Italy's most historic clubs.

Serie A records

Most appearances (all seasons)

Gianluigi Buffon - **657 games**

Most goals (all seasons)

Silvio Piola - **274**

Most goals (in one seasons)

Gino Rossetti (Torino), Gonzalo Higuaín (Napoli), and Ciro Immobile (Lazio) – 36

Did you know?

As well as a trophy, the winning team wears the scudetto badge on their shirts the season after their victory. The badge is a small shield with the colors of the flag of Italy.

Number of teams	20
Number of games each season	38
Clubs relegated each season	3

Leading the way

Juventus have won more Serie A titles than any other club (36). They have been runners-up a record 21 times too. Their name "Juventus" may mean "youth", but their nickname is the "Old Lady."

Goalkeeper Gianluigi Buffon won Serie A a record ten times with Juventus.

Serie A Femminile

Italy's highest women's league is called Serie A for short. It was founded in 1968, although it only became fully professional for the 2022–23 season. The season is split into two parts. First, all ten teams play each other home and away, before the table is split in two. The top five teams play each other twice more, as do the bottom five teams.

Patrizia Panico is the league's all-time top goal scorer. She played for eight different clubs in Serie A.

Number of teams	12
Number of games each season	28
Clubs relegated each season	1-2

Serie A Femminile records

Most titles (all seasons)

Torres – 7

Most goals (all seasons)

Patrizia Panico – 600+

Roma celebrate winning their second Serie A title at the end of the 2023–24 season.

Ligue 1

France has had a professional league since the 1932–33 season, when 20 teams competed in a league called National and then Division 1. In 2002, the league changed its name again to Ligue 1.

Classic clubs

Only three founding member clubs still play in France's top league, almost one hundred years later—Marseille, Nice, and Rennes.

Number of teams	18
Number of games each season	34
Clubs relegated each season	4

Paris Saint-Germain (in the navy kit) is the league's most successful team.

Ligue 1 records

Most appearances (all seasons)

Mickaël Landreau – **618 games**

Most goals (all seasons)

Delio Onnis – **299**

Most goals (in one seasons)

Josip Skoblar (Olympique de Marseille) - **44**

Did you know?

When Paris Saint-Germain bought Brazil forward Neymar Jr. from FC Barcelona in 2017, his fee of €222 million (about $250 million) made him the most expensive player in history.

Première Ligue

France's top league for women has existed for more than 50 seasons. It became known as the Première Ligue for 2024–25, when play-offs were contested between the top four clubs at the end of the season. Olympique Lyonnais (Lyon) have ruled the league over the past two decades.

Lyon won an unbeaten 14 titles in a row between 2006 and 2020.

Number of teams	12
Number of games each season	22
Clubs relegated each season	2

Première Ligue records

Most league titles

Olympique Lyonnais – 17

Most goals (in one seasons)

Sandrine Brétigny – 42

Did you know?

The Première Ligue attracts top players from abroad. USA midfielder Crystal Dunn (front row, middle) and ex-England goalkeeper Mary Earps (back row, third from left) both star for Paris Saint-Germain.

Major League Soccer

Major League Soccer (MLS) is the leading league in the United States. Thirty teams make up the league, with 27 in the United States and three from Canada. They are divided between the Western and Eastern Conferences. Play began in 1996. Unlike most top leagues in soccer, MLS does not have promotion or relegation.

Number of teams	30
Number of games each season	34

The gleaming MLS Cup.

Two trophies

Clubs in the Eastern and Western Conferences try to win a trophy called the Supporters' Shield by earning the most points. The league's top 16 teams then compete in the play-offs for the prize of the MLS Cup.

Captain Lionel Messi and his Inter Miami team celebrate winning their first Supporters' Shield in 2024.

MLS records

Most appearances (all seasons)

Nick Rimando - 514 games

Most goals (all seasons)

Chris Wondolowski – 171

Most goals (in one season)

Carlos Vela (Los Angeles FC) - 34

National Women's Soccer League

The top women's league in the United States is known as the NWSL for short. Its first season kicked off in 2013, although two professional leagues existed before this time. Like the men's league (MLS), a play-off tournament takes place at the end of the season, after a Shield champion has been crowned.

The style of soccer played in the NWSL is based on strength and speed.

NWSL records

Most appearances (all seasons)

Lauren Barnes – 232+ games

Most goals (all seasons)

Lynn Biyendolo (was Williams) – 80

Most goals (in one season)

Temwa Chawinga (Kansas City Current) – 20

Number of teams	14*
Number of games each season	26**

Third trophy

The Shield winners then play the winners of the Championship (the playoff tournament) in a single cup competition called the NWSL Challenge Cup.

*Starting in 2026, 16 NWSL teams will make up the league. **As of March 2025.

The Champions League

The top clubs from Europe's strongest leagues proudly compete in the Champions League. It is the most-watched club competition in the world. The tournament was first held in 1955, when it was called the European Cup and was won by Spanish club Real Madrid.

European giants Real Madrid claimed a record fifteenth Champions League title in 2024.

Champions League records

Most appearances (all seasons)

Cristiano Ronaldo – 183 games

Most goals (all seasons)

Cristiano Ronaldo – 140

Most goals (in one season)

Cristiano Ronaldo – 17

Number of teams	36
Number of games each season	up to 17

Competition changes

In 2024–25, the group stage changed to a single competition with all 36 teams competing in one giant league.

*Played by the two finalists in the 2024–25 season.

The Women's Champions League

A competition for the top women's clubs in Europe was first staged in 2001–02, when it was called the "UEFA Women's Cup". It became the Women's Champions League in 2009–10. Every season, memorable matches are played in this **elite** competition to decide the best women's club in Europe.

Number of teams	18
Number of games each season	9*

History-makers

Olympique Lyonnais Féminin (Lyon Women) are the most successful club in the competition's history. They have won the trophy eight times, including a record five titles in a row from 2016 to 2020.

Big rivals

Barcelona have been Lyon's biggest rivals in recent years. The Spanish club won their first title in 2021 and have since added two more trophies.

Barcelona captain Alexia Putellas lifts the Women's Champions League trophy in 2024.

Women's Champions League records

Most appearances (all seasons)

Wendie Renard – **124 games** **

Most goals (all seasons)

Ada Hegerberg – **66****

Most goals (in one season)

Ada Hegerberg – **15**

*Played by the two finalists in the 2024–25 season.
**As of March 2025.

Cup competitions

Some of the most exciting soccer games take place in cup competitions, where small clubs get the chance to take on bigger and richer clubs. Games can be full of drama and comebacks, ending in shock results that are remembered for years to come.

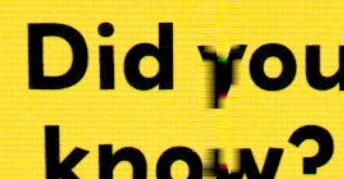

Did you know?

Everton's Louis Saha holds the record for the fastest goal in an FA Cup final. It took him just 25 seconds to score.

The FA Cup

The FA Cup is the oldest national soccer competition in the world. The first final was played in 1872. Arsenal holds the record for the most victories. Their first trophy came in 1930.

FA Cup records

Most wins (club)	
Men's Arsenal - 14	Women's Arsenal - 14

Most wins (players)	
Men's Ashley Cole (Arsenal and Chelsea) – 7	Women's Rachel Yankey (Arsenal and Fulham) – 11

Most wins (coach)	
Men's Arsène Wenger (Arsenal) – 7	Women's Vic Akers (Arsenal) – 10

The FA Cup trophy is decorated with ribbons in the colors of the winning team.

The Copa del Rey

The "King's Cup" is one of the most famous cup competitions in Europe. It is the oldest competition in Spanish football. The first trophy was won in 1903. The women's version is called the Copa de la Reina or the "Queen's Cup."

Copa del Rey / de la Reina records

Most wins (club)

Men's	Women's
Barcelona – 32	Barcelona – 10

Copa Libertadores records

Most wins (club)

Men's	Women's
Independiente (Argentina) – 7	Corinthians (Brazil) – 5

The Copa Libertadores

The men's cup has been contested by South America's top clubs every year since 1960. Players and fans from Uruguay, Argentina, Brazil, and beyond dream of winning this special trophy. 32 teams take part in the men's cup, while 16 teams play in the women's cup. The Copa Libertadores Femenina first played out in 2009.

Real Madrid recorded a record score of 5–3 when they beat Al-Hilal in the 2022 final.

The Club World Cup

FIFA's Club World Cup is a competition that decides the best club in the world. 32 clubs from around the globe take part. Brazilian club Corinthians won the first Club World Cup in 2000 in a penalty shootout.

Club World Cup records

Most wins (club)

Real Madrid – 5

More soccer!

As soccer continues to grow around the world, it inspires other versions of the game. Here are some more ways that more players and fans enjoy getting involved in the sport.

Futsal

The game of Futsal was invented in Uruguay and Brazil in South America in the 1930s. It is played indoors on a hard court. The ball used is smaller, heavier, and less bouncy than a normal soccer ball. Five players make up each team. Futsal has had its own World Cup since 1989.

Futsal World Cup records

Most wins

Brazil – 6

Most appearances

Argentina, Brazil, and Spain – 10

Brazil claimed their sixth World Cup victory in 2024, at the Futsal World Cup in Uzbekistan.

Did you know?

Famous soccer players Lionel Messi and Neymar Jr. both developed their excellent technique and ball control by playing futsal growing up.

Beach Soccer World Cup records

Most wins

Brazil – 7

Most appearances

Brazil and Japan – 12

Brazil beat Italy in the final of the Beach Soccer World Cup 2024 in the United Arab Emirates.

Beach soccer

Beach soccer is played barefoot on a small pitch made of sand. Like Futsal, teams are five-a-side with no limits on the number of substitutes. Games last 36 minutes and are split into three thirds of 12 minutes.

Disability soccer

Competitions such as the Paralympic Games allow players with the same disability to compete on the big stage. Blind soccer is a five-a-side game for players with visual impairments. The ball makes a sound when it moves so that players can follow it.

Besides blind soccer, there are international competitions for those with other disabilities to enjoy the beautiful game. Versions include cerebral palsy, amputee, frame, powerchair, and deaf soccer.

France and Argentina played out the blind soccer final at the Paralympic Games in 2024. France won their first gold medal.

Esports

Did you know that there is a World Cup for gamers? Some of the world's best video gamers represent their country each year at the FIFAe World Cup. Indonesia won the console trophy and Malaysia won the mobile trophy in 2024.

Team Indonesia show off their trophy at the FIFAe World Cup in 2024.

Glossary

amateur
A person or team that takes part in a sport without being paid.

assist
A pass that leads directly to a goal being scored.

attacker
Any player on the pitch whose job it is to score or assist goals.

clean sheet
When a team and its goalkeeper don't let in any goals over a whole match.

CONCACAF
One of the six groups of countries (confederations) in world soccer. It represents national teams from North America, Central America, and the Caribbean region.

confederation
A group of countries that work together to look after soccer and organize tournaments in a particular region.

continental
Belonging or relating to one of the seven continents in the world.

cross
A pass made in the air or on the ground, often from wide areas into the penalty box.

defender
Players who play in the area between the goalkeeper and the midfielders.

dribble
To move the ball up the field, keeping it close to the body and taking lots of touches.

elite
The very best or highest-level teams, players, or competitions.

formation
The way a team is set up on the field. The number of players in defense, midfield, and attack change for different formations. The goalkeeper is not included.

forward
Players who play farthest up the field. They try to score or assist goals.

full-time
The end of a match. A period of extra time can be played after this if needed.

goalkeeper
The only player who can handle the ball in their own penalty area on each team. Their job is to stop goals being scored against them.

halftime
The break in between the two halves of a match. In a 90-minute match, halftime lasts 15 minutes.

kickoff
The pass made from the center spot at the start of a match or after a goal has been scored.

midfielder
Players who play in the middle of the field, between the defenders and the attackers.

opposition
The other team in a game. Also called "opponents."

outfield
All players except for the goalkeeper.

pass
When a player moves the ball toward a teammate using their feet, head, or chest.

playoff
A final contest, often between two teams over two games, home and away.

possession
When one team has control of the ball and holds on to it by passing it around their opponents.

professional
A person or team that gets paid to play, earning enough money for it to be their job.

red card
Shown by the referee to a player who has seriously broken the rules, meaning they have to leave the game.

referee
The person in charge of a game. They make sure it follows the laws of the game.

relegation
To drop down to a lower division at the end of the season, after finishing in last place or among the bottom teams.

rivals
Two teams that compete fiercely against each other. Players and fans take the competition very seriously.

shoot
To aim a kick at goal, usually while in the attacking half of the field.

stadium
A large structure used for outdoor sports with a field in the middle and seating for fans.

striker
The forward who plays farthest up the field. Their main job is to score goals.

substitute
A player who joins the game after it has started. They replace an injured or tired teammate or try to change the game tactics.

tactics
The plan or actions that a coach or team chooses when playing a game.

touchlines
The lines that mark the longest two sides of a soccer field.

winger
A wide midfielder who plays close to the touchline on one side of the pitch. They make crosses into the attacking penalty area.

yellow card
A warning shown by the referee to a player who has broken a law of the game.

Index

CBF
BRASIL
7